Tomorrow's World

The ROBOT AGE

Graham Storrs

The Bookwright Press
New York · 1985

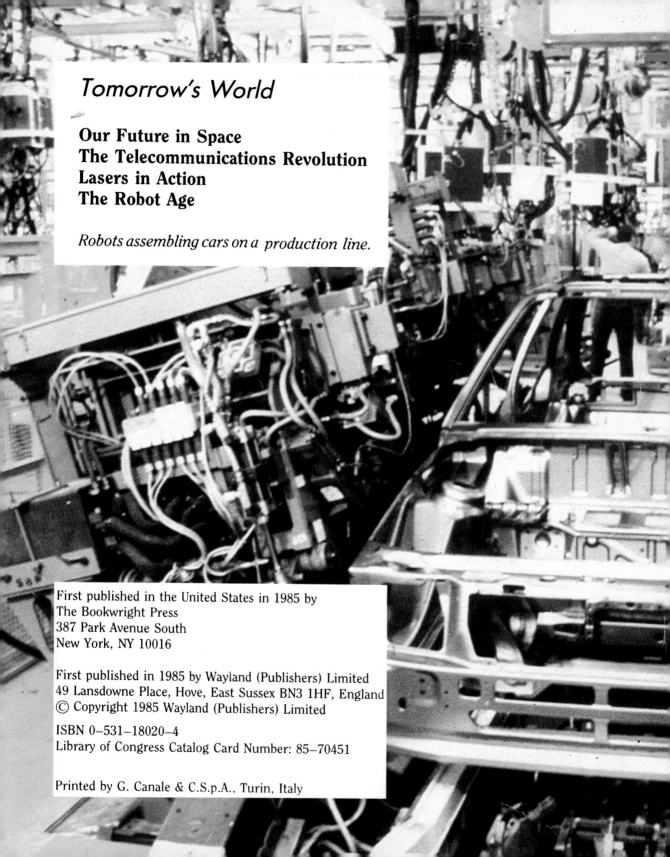

Tomorrow's World

Our Future in Space
The Telecommunications Revolution
Lasers in Action
The Robot Age

Robots assembling cars on a production line.

First published in the United States in 1985 by
The Bookwright Press
387 Park Avenue South
New York, NY 10016

First published in 1985 by Wayland (Publishers) Limited
49 Lansdowne Place, Hove, East Sussex BN3 1HF, England
© Copyright 1985 Wayland (Publishers) Limited

ISBN 0–531–18020–4
Library of Congress Catalog Card Number: 85–70451

Printed by G. Canale & C.S.p.A., Turin, Italy

Contents

The story of robots

A robot is a machine that can be taught, or programmed, to work for us. Most robots in use today can imitate some human actions, such as movement, but (unlike the robots in movies) they neither look like humans nor behave much like them.

Most robots in use in factories today are jointed arms something like these.

However, we are just entering an age when machines that have a sense of touch, and can see, and hear, that can speak, think and learn, will take over the work that, until recently, only people could do. As robots become "smarter," and as they become more widespread, we could well see the biggest changes in our lives that we have ever known.

The universal robot

For centuries people have dreamed of having a perfect slave, a robot worker to do their work for them. Only now has the technology which is needed to build one reached a sufficiently advanced stage. But the dream has not always been a happy one. The idea of a machine-person is rather frightening to most people, and many stories have been written about robot servants that threaten their owners. The word "robot" itself was first used to describe mechanical workers in the play *R.U.R.* ("Rossum's Universal

Robots") which was written in the 1920s by the Czech dramatist, Karel Capek. In this play the robots finally turn on their masters and destroy them. Other fictional robots have been less menacing, especially those written about by the science fiction writer Isaac Asimov. In the course of a long series of stories his robots lead the world into a golden age of peace and prosperity.

The real robots of the 1980s are very different from anything these writers have imagined. Instead of the human-like, super-intelligent machines they foresaw, we have very odd looking machines, designed to perform a fairly narrow range of tasks. They do not look like people; they are mostly deaf, dumb and blind; they cannot move around easily, and they need a computer to give them what little intelligence they have! Yet from these small beginnings we can expect to see rapid and dramatic growth in the abilities of the robots of the future.

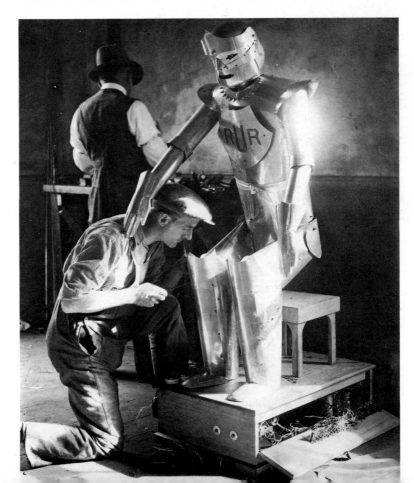

Inspired by ideas from science fiction, an English inventor created this robot in 1928. It could speak, answer questions and shake hands.

Robots are still popular in science fiction. These famous robots, C-3PO and R2-D2, are here seen during the making of the film Return of the Jedi. *Both parts were in fact played by actors.*

Ancient automata

In ancient times people made mechanical devices which resembled people or animals and did clever things. Almost 2,000 years ago, Hero of Alexandria is said to have built mechanical birds which sang and drank and even flew! More recently, in the eighteenth century, mechanical figures were made which played chess or spoke or did similarly astonishing things. These machines were known as automata, because they worked automatically. The most popular were those which could write or play musical instruments.

In the late eighteenth century, a Swiss clockmaker named Pierre Jacquet-Droz made some of the most famous automata. One is a music-making doll that plays on a keyboard. As she plays, her chest moves in and out as though she is breathing and her head nods in time to the music. Jacquet-Droz also made a model of a child writing at a desk. The child dips his pen in an inkwell, shakes off the excess ink and then writes in the best handwriting. The clockwork inside can be adjusted to change the words the child writes.

Later still, in 1870, an engineer called George Moore built a mechanical man. The figure looked like a man in armor and was driven by a steam engine inside. It could walk at 14 kph (9 mph) with steam coming from its mouth through a vent disguised to look like a cigar!

But these automata were really just mechanical toys. A great deal of scientific research had to be done before our modern robots could be developed.

This automaton was made by Jacquet-Droz in the eighteenth century.

Machines that can be programmed

One of the first machines ever to be controlled by a stored program was a loom designed to weave patterned silk. It was invented by a Frenchman, Joseph Jacquard, in 1801. A program is a set of instructions for doing a job. The program for the Jacquard loom was stored on cards with holes punched in them. This meant that the loom would weave any pattern that was desired simply by using a different set of punched cards. It also meant that even an unskilled weaver could produce cloth that had once required great skill and patience to produce.

The idea of using stored programs was taken up in the 1820s by Charles Babbage when he invented the first mechanical computer, and the idea is central to modern digital computers. Punched cards, punched tapes and, recently, magnetic tapes and disks have frequently been

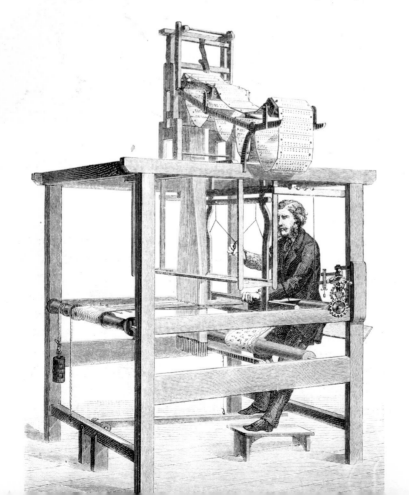

The Jacquard loom, which could be "programmed" to weave different patterns. The "program" is stored on the punched cards.

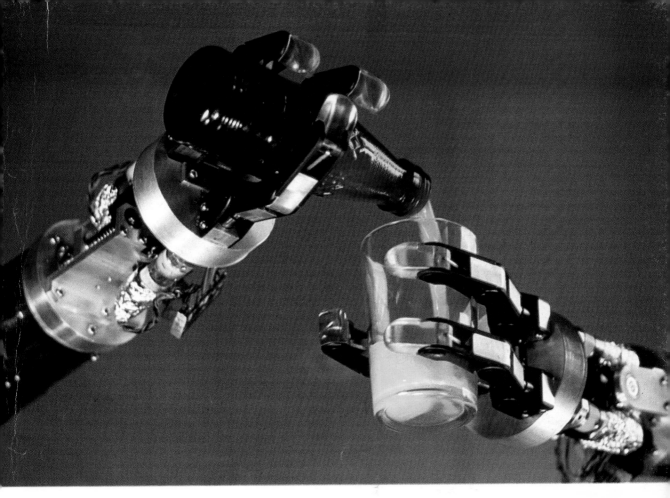

Information from these robot hands is fed back to a computer. This "feedback" of information helps the robot to pour the drink without spilling any.

used to control machinery. Today's robots would not be possible without the stored programs which guide their movements.

Feedback

Another idea which has become central to the development of robotics is "feedback." Try drawing a picture with your eyes closed and you will find it almost impossible. This is because you need to see what your hand is doing in order to control it properly. In other words, you need "feedback." Information about the position of the hand must be fed back, through the eyes, to the brain so that the correct control signals can be sent to the muscles which move the hand. In the same way, robots must have some method of monitoring their own behavior before they can perform even simple tasks, such as picking up an object.

The invention of the silicon chip has played an important part in the development of robots. The matchstick in this picture shows you just how tiny the chip is.

Making robots possible

There are many other developments that have added to the knowledge needed to build robots. For example, in engineering there has been the invention of power sources such as hydraulics, pneumatics and electric motors and solenoids (a kind of electric piston); ways of controlling power with flywheels and regulators; and ways of transmitting power through pulleys, levers, gears and drive shafts. From the early days of experiments with electricity, research has led to the development of digital electronics and the computer. A host of other achievements, such as the development of programming languages and electro-mechanical sensors, the production of metals and plastics, and changes in manufacturing methods, have all helped to make today's robots possible.

This early computer, built in Manchester, England, in the 1940s, filled a whole room.

What is a robot?

There are many kinds of robots. Some do heavy lifting and stacking jobs in factories. Some use tools such as welding torches and paint sprays. Others guide weapons, forklift trucks or buses. There are even robots to shear sheep or check that there are enough chocolate chips in cookies!

Robots range in size from the "turtles" that scuttle about the classroom floor, and small desktop "arms" for light assembly work, to large floor-mounted arms that can easily lift a car. They also vary in appearance. A robot may look like a truck, a many-jointed metal arm, a six-legged metal spider, an aircraft, a snake, or even a person. What they

This robot arm can move small items by picking them up, swiveling around, and then putting them down in another place.

all have in common is that they are machines, capable of being programmed or taught to do various useful jobs of work.

Most robots work in factories. These are mainly the jointed-arm type of robot. They spend their time either picking up things and moving them to another place, or using tools which they hold in their "hands."

Basically, a robot is a machine much like any other. It is made of metal and plastic and is driven by motors and pistons. However, two things make a robot a very special kind of machine. First, they can be programmed and controlled by computers; and, second, many of them can sense the world around them or their own movements with special electrical or mechanical sensors.

Robot arms assembling Mercedes-Benz cars.

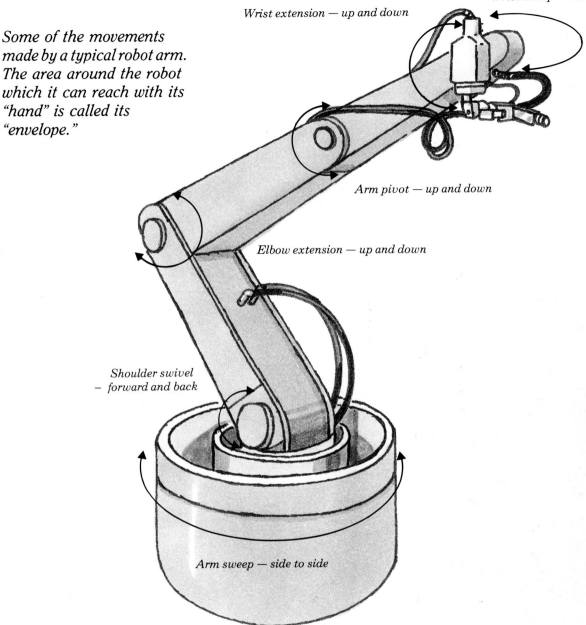

Some of the movements made by a typical robot arm. The area around the robot which it can reach with its "hand" is called its "envelope."

Wrist sweep — side to side

Wrist extension — up and down

Arm pivot — up and down

Elbow extension — up and down

Shoulder swivel — forward and back

Arm sweep — side to side

Robot arms

The most common type of robot used in industry is the robot arm. These arms may be powered by electric motors but the most powerful use hydraulics and work very much like the "arms" on the mechanical diggers used on building sites. There are many kinds of robot arm. The various types have different shapes for their working "envelopes." (The

envelope of a robot is the area around it that it can reach with its "hand.") The shape of this area depends on the way the joints in the arm can move.

Some arms can bend and twist like a snake or a spine. Some turn around a central pillar, with an arm that swivels up and down and telescopes in and out. They move rather like the turret on a tank. This kind of robot has a spherical envelope. An arm which can move up and down, left and right and in and out is sometimes known as an XYZ robot (one letter for each kind of movement). Another kind of robot arm moves up and down a central pillar, and rotates and telescopes in and out. Its envelope is the shape of a cylinder.

One of the most common types of robot, though, is the jointed-arm robot. This is fixed to the floor like all the others but it can bend much like a human arm, at the shoulder, elbow and wrist. Some can bend the central pillar too as if they were bending at the waist. The wrist on a

A robot arm programmed to spray the bodywork of TV sets.

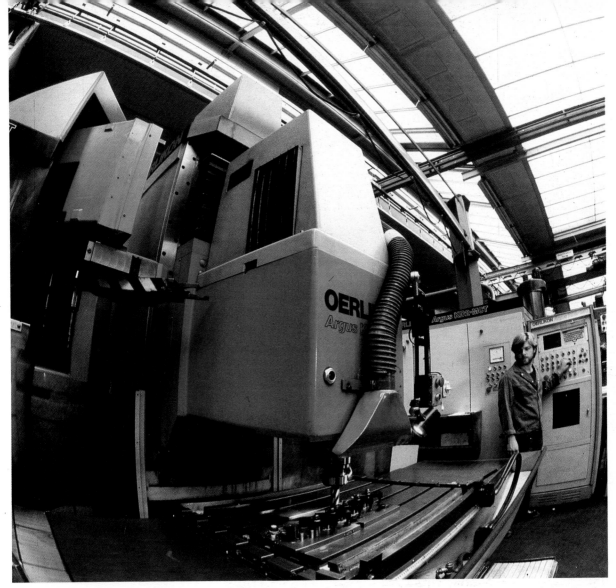

This huge drilling machine can be operated by just one man at the computer controls.

robot arm is the most complicated part since it must be able to bend in many directions and rotate too, just like our own wrists.

Some robots are made like arms so that they can lift and carry things just as a person would. For this reason they are called robot manipulators. They can be used to hold engine parts in place for a grinding tool, say, or to pass parts from a conveyor belt into boxes. They can also hold tools or have tools fitted to them so that they can weld or spray paint or tighten screws.

15

Left *Robot transporters carrying components around a factory, their paths guided by wires in the floor.*

Mobile robots

Robots that can be given the ability to move around are known as mobile robots. In a factory these robots are used as automatic forklift trucks and as simple "shuttles" for moving goods around. They usually work by following a trail on the ground. This could be a painted line but it is more often a buried electric cable which they can detect with special sensors. Robot buses are being built which will follow cables buried under the roads and automatically stop at bus stops to let passengers on and off.

The big problem for a mobile robot is to get where it is going without bumping into things along the way. Because most of them cannot see at all, they follow their trails blindly. Bumpers around their sides act as touch sensors to stop them if they are about to hit anything. Some mobile robots use sonar or infrared detectors to warn them of obstacles, bouncing a beam of sound or light off anything in their path and stopping when the reflections get too close.

Below *A mobile robot waiter serving food and drink in a restaurant.*

Some mobile robots can navigate by having maps programmed into them. If the robot knows where it started from, it can measure the distances it travels and remember the turns it makes so that it can always work out its exact position on the map. These robots still need touch or echo sensors to alert them to any obstacles in their path.

Because mobile robots work mainly in factories, they need to be able to turn in a very small space. They usually do this by turning the wheels or tracks on opposite sides of the vehicle at different speeds, just like a tank or a bulldozer. A robot can turn right around on the spot by turning opposite wheels in opposite directions. Turtles and "buggies" and other toy robots use this same method.

A robot with wheels like a car. It was designed by American scientists to inspect and repair nuclear rockets too dangerous for people to approach.

How robots learn

A robot learns by being programmed, just like a computer. In fact, in every robot (or connected to it) there is a computer which controls its movements. Without a program to tell it what to do, a robot could not do anything at all.

Walk-through teaching

If we wanted to teach a robot how to open a window, there are four ways we could go about it. The first is to show it by holding its "hand" and moving it through all the steps necessary: reaching out, taking hold of the handle, turning the handle, pushing the window open, letting go of the handle and bringing its hand back. The robot would record

A large floor-mounted arm being "taught" how to perform a task.

every movement that each of its joints made while it was being taught and then, when it was given the signal, it would play back the movements exactly as they happened the first time, just like a tape recorder for movements. This kind of "walk-through" or "lead-through" teaching is especially useful for teaching skills like paint spraying and welding.

A machine spraying car bodies with paint. It has been taught to do just what human paint sprayers do.

Teaching pendants

Another way to teach a robot is by using a remote control device called a teaching pendant. This is a box attached to the robot's computer, with switches that operate the motors in each of its joints. Using these switches, the robot arm is moved to each position for the job it is being taught and then a "record" button is pressed so that it will remember that position. When it has learned every position, the robot can then run through them all in the right sequence to do the job.

A more complicated way of teaching a robot is by writing a computer program, in a special language, to tell it how to move each of its parts. A language called Logo is often used to teach people about robots. It is especially designed to control simple mobile robots such as the turtle. It contains instructions such as FORWARD 10 RIGHT 90 (meaning "go forward ten units and then turn 90 degrees to the right"). For industrial robots there are much more complicated languages such as Clare, AML and APT.

Using their brains . . .

Finally, robots can learn by working a problem out for themselves. Very few robots have yet been built which are "smart" enough to do this, and they have all been experimental devices which needed enormous computer power. A famous early experiment along these lines involved a robot called Shakey. Built in the 1960s by researchers at Stanford University, Shakey could move blocks around and find its way around a room, avoiding obstacles which it could "see" with a TV camera. It could even find an electric socket and recharge itself! This kind of machine intelligence is very hard to achieve. Scientists studying artificial intelligence are only just beginning to understand the problems involved. However, it is likely that, in the future, more and more robots will be able to discover what to do for themselves without needing to be taught.

A jointed arm robot being programmed using a personal computer and a special computer language.

Robot senses

Many of today's robots have only very limited sensory abilities. A robot that has been taught, using lead-through or a similar technique, to pick up plastic parts from a conveyor belt and put them into boxes, will just as happily go through the motions if the conveyor belt breaks down and no parts are arriving. It will also just as blindly drop

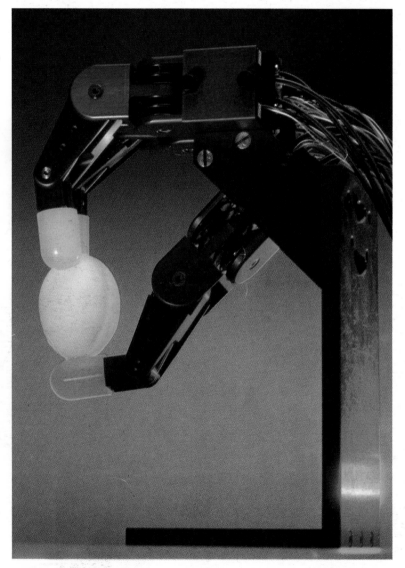

Left An experimental robot gripper holding an egg to demonstrate just how carefully it can be controlled.

Right Another kind of robot hand (top) and robot arms designed to handle dangerous radioactive material (below).

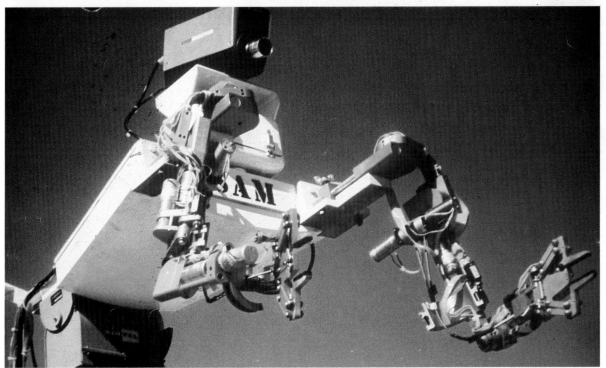

parts onto the floor if the box to put them in is not where it should be! This is because such robots have no way of knowing what is going on around them. They have no senses.

Giving a robot senses makes it much more useful and adaptable to different jobs. Imagine a robot which has to reach out and grasp a small machine part. If the part is not just where it should be, or even if it is lying the wrong way around, the robot will fail. This is why factories which use robots go to a great deal of trouble to ensure that every tool and part the robot needs is in exactly the right position for it and that the robot's actions are perfectly in time with the other machines with which it works. Giving the robot some simple senses can make it far more reliable.

The dog on the left is very much smarter than the toy dog on the right. Robots of the future, however, will be given senses so that they can see, speak, think and learn.

In touch with the world

A sense of touch is one of the first senses that robots have been given. Strain gauges and microswitches can be built into a robot's hand and wrist so that it can "feel" what it is doing. If a robot's grippers can sense when they have touched something, they can be used to hold very delicate objects without breaking them. Also, if they can feel the pressure they exert when they push or pull at things, they can be programmed to cope with more haphazard arrangements of the things they must handle.

Robot arms can also be given "proximity" sensors to tell when objects are close to their hands. These often work

This robot is a brilliant chess player, but it can do nothing else!

by sending a beam out from one side of the hand and detecting it at the other when it bounces back. Sound, infrared and laser beams are often used for this. Robots can even be given a crude sense of sight. Television cameras can be used to pick up images of the work the robot is doing, and computer programs then pick out the shapes of objects in the picture and guide the robot to grasp them.

Giving senses to robots is a very complicated matter. The problem is that extremely intelligent computer programs are needed to understand what a camera is "seeing" or a microphone is "hearing" and scientists have not yet learned how to write such smart programs. However, the research goes on all the time and it will not be long before advanced robot vision systems are commonplace on the factory floor. When this happens, robots will be able to move from the carefully controlled factory environment into the far more complicated world outside, in the streets and in the home.

Robots are controlled by computers, which act as their "brains."

Robot brains

The "brain" of a robot is the computer that controls it. A computer stores information about what the robot should do and when it should do it and it then sends signals out to the motors that drive the robot so that it does what it is supposed to. Leading a robot through even a fairly straightforward task, such as welding a bicycle frame, generates thousands of readings from position sensors in its joints. The computer remembers all of these by writing them onto magnetic disks. It can then read the data on the disks and pass it on to the robot to enable it to do the job.

If the robot was taught with a teaching pendant, or was programmed with a robotic programming language, the computer must work out how and where to move the robot. This involves the computer in lots of very fast arithmetic. The computer is constantly monitoring any sensors that the robot might have (such as the touch-sensitive bumpers on a robot truck) so that if it gets a signal from one it can make the robot take appropriate action.

Robots working for us

In the early days of the human race, our ancestors struggled to find food and shelter. They learned to farm and to build, but life was always a grueling and wearying toil. In order to live, people had to work and struggle – unless they could get other people to do the work for them.

Most of the so-called "great societies" of the past, including the Greeks and the Romans, were slave societies. Slaves were held under threat of beatings or death and made to do the hard labor and the menial tasks. This gave the ruling classes freedom from toil so that they could devote their time to philosophy, the arts and the sciences for which those societies are famous.

A dream of the future – or a nightmare? This Russian robot policeman from the 1960s was only an actor in disguise.

Robot workers never get tired, or bored, or make a careless mistake.

The great promise of robotics is that it can give us the benefits of a slave society (freedom to be creative, while reaping the fruits of someone else's labor) without the need to enslave people. It seems almost too good to be true, and yet the technologies which can make it possible are already starting to appear.

Into production

For many years, factories which assemble machines (such as cars, for example) have used production line methods. This means that groups of workers each do one small part of the work, perhaps bolting on a particular piece or painting some part. The machine then passes to another small group, perhaps on a conveyor belt, for the next piece to be added. People who work on these production lines find the work very boring and unpleasant because they have only one simple task to do and they do it over and over again, perhaps hundreds or even thousands of times every day.

Fortunately, this is exactly the kind of work that robots are best suited to. Although they break down occasionally, robots never become tired or bored. They can be taught simple tasks, such as welding two parts together, tightening screws, painting with a spray gun, or moving a part from one spot to another, and they can repeat these tasks

endlessly. Because car making can easily be organized for a production line, many car factories now use robots instead of people. The car bodies and other parts move along a conveyor belt and dozens of robots, arranged along each side, work on them as they move past, their movements synchronized (timed) with the speed of the conveyor.

The robot which does this kind of work is usually a single large arm with some kind of "hand" or tool on the end. These robot arms have as much maneuverability as a sitting person (although many are much larger and stronger than people) and they can be taught to do a wide variety of jobs. So the same type of robot may be welding with a laser beam in one part of the factory, packing boxes in another, and bolting machine parts together in another.

Above *Adhesive being applied to car doors by a robot arm.*

Right *The cockpit of a modern passenger plane. The newest automatic pilot systems can make a plane take off, fly and land without the human pilot touching the controls.*

Some robots move around the factory floor carrying parts or stacking up the finished car bodies. They look like small trucks or forklifts and they follow set routes according to the programs they have been given.

Robots in control

Sometimes experts use the term "robotic device" to refer to a mechanical or electrical system which controls power or machinery. An early example of such a device is the steam governor which keeps steam driven engines running at a steady speed. Modern robotic devices are much more flexible and programmable.

One of the best-known examples is the automatic pilot that is fitted in most large aircraft. This allows the human pilot to preset a particular course which the plane will then automatically follow.

This remotely-controlled helicopter carries a TV camera. It can be used as a security guard, to protect property, or as a kind of "spy in the sky."

Cruise missiles are robotic flying weapons capable of steering themselves round obstacles.

The automatic pilot is a computer program which monitors the aircraft's instruments. Information about the aircraft's direction, speed, height and so on is fed into the computer. The computer then adjusts the controls to keep the airplane on course.

The newest automatic pilots can also take care of changes in course which can be preprogrammed by the pilot. Recently, even more complex automatic pilots have been introduced into some large airliners. They can use information from radio beacons at airports to help them control the aircraft throughout takeoff and landing. This means that the automatic pilot could take off, fly a complicated route, and land the aircraft at another airport without the human pilot ever touching the controls! This device can transform the airplane into a sophisticated flying robot.

War machines

Even more elaborate technology is used to control the new generation of flying weapons (such as cruise missiles). These robot weapons have control systems which keep them flying on course, using internal electronic "maps" and taking bearings from orbiting space satellites to check their position. They also use radar sensors to detect any obstacles in their path and so steer around them.

On the ground, there are many experiments now taking place to develop robot tanks and mobile guns and missile launchers. Controlling a robot on the ground is much more difficult than it is in the air because extra senses and extra intelligence are needed for the machine to understand its surroundings. The weapon needs to be able to tell what kind of ground it can and cannot cross, how to tell a target (such as a tank) from a non-target (such as a tractor) and how to tell a friend from a foe!

Because the ground can be so rough to cross, armies are looking at the possibility of using robots that travel on legs rather than wheels or tracks. They would be used for jobs such as sentry duty, or for dangerous assignments like mine sweeping and reconnoitering enemy territory. One robot being considered in this role is a six-legged walking robot which can carry a variety of devices on a platform above its legs.

A bomb-detecting robot, like this one, can help protect humans from danger.

In dangerous places

One of the great benefits of robot workers is that they can be used in environments which are so harsh and dangerous that people would risk their lives by working in them. Mining for coal, metals or minerals is one such dangerous job where people are constantly exposed to hazards such as cave-ins, flooding, gas explosions and radiation. People in these jobs often work in very poor conditions, sometimes

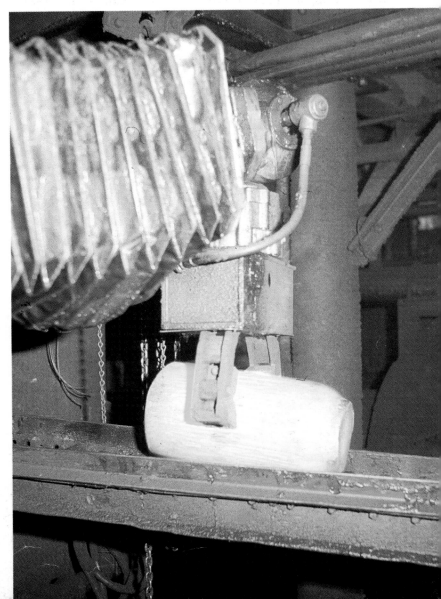

A robot hand designed to hold red-hot metal.

hot, damp, badly lit and cramped. They may also be exposed to dust in the air which can leave them with permanently damaged lungs. The development of mining machinery has greatly improved conditions for miners but the introduction of newly developed mining robots promises to free people forever from this unpleasant work.

This undersea research vessel has robot arms and can travel safely in the hostile depths of the sea.

Under the sea

The quest for oil to fuel our society has driven people to sink wells far out at sea. Gigantic oil production platforms stand off the coasts of many countries and people must dive to great depths, at great risk to themselves, to maintain and repair the rigs and the pipelines which carry the oil and gas from them. Robot divers now exist which can do some of this dangerous work. They are small robot submarines, remotely controlled from the surface, with a jointed robot arm fixed to the front.

An artist's impression of Deepstar, *another* *underwater explorer.*

Robots in space

One of the most famous robot arms must be the one used by the Space Shuttle to carry satellites out of its cargo hold and into space. Yet this is by no means the only use of robots in space. A spacecraft in flight needs to make many tiny adjustments to its course with a speed and accuracy impossible for a human pilot. So spacecraft are

The Space Shuttle's robot arm under construction in a laboratory.

fitted with robotic devices like the automatic pilots used in airplanes.

Robots are especially useful in space exploration. Because of the great distances and hostile environments, it takes too long and it is too dangerous to send people far out into space. The distance also makes radio control of spacecraft difficult because signals take so long to travel so far. Robot probes such as the Mars Lander, launched in 1975 to study the soil and atmosphere of Mars, are the obvious answer to these problems. It is almost certain that future exploration of other planets will be by similar robot spacecraft and not by people.

A photograph of Mars, taken from the surface by the robot Mars Lander.

Robots for everyone?

One of the greatest triumphs of our century, and one often taken for granted, is the mechanization of housework. Keeping a home and its occupants at a reasonable level of cleanliness and comfort is a tedious and laborious task. Electromechanical devices such as washing machines, food processors, vacuum cleaners, dishwashers and tumble dryers, as well as gas or electric appliances like stoves and electric irons, have taken a lot of the hard work out of housework. Yet it still remains one of the most labor-intensive of jobs.

Topo, a "personal robot," is driven by a home computer. He can be made to talk, move around the house, and carry objects from room to room.

A robot nurse pushing a baby carriage. This machine was made by a Japanese toy company. It will be a long time before machines replace humans at this kind of activity.

Household robots

Many people hope that the new science of robotics will finally remove the burden of housework from our shoulders. But housework is probably one of the last areas of work that will be effectively robotized. For housework is not just one job but dozens of jobs; the skills that a robot would require just to make a bed are nothing like those needed to cook a meal. In turn these are different from the skills needed to sweep the floor. To make a robot that could do housework would mean building a general-purpose machine with human-like senses and human-like intelligence. Unfortunately, robotics is a long way from building such devices.

It is more likely that domestic work will be done by a large number of different, specialist robots, perhaps looking something like the machines they will replace. So the lawn will be mowed by a grass-cutting robot, the floors

cleaned by a floor-scrubbing robot, and so on. A table-clearing robot has already been developed as an experiment and there are simple robot "butlers" which serve drinks at conferences, but there is still a lot of research to be done. Of course, with all these robots around the house, people may find their homes getting rather crowded!

Turtles

Some years ago, Seymour Papert (an American scientist) helped develop a simple programming language which he called Logo. He used it to teach programming ideas to young children. The language is used to control a small robot, called a turtle, which moves around the floor drawing lines with a pen. The language and the robots became popular in schools and have recently become available for enthusiasts to buy to run from their microcomputers.

Personal robots

All kinds of other small mobile robots are now becoming available for use at home. Most have touch sensors and can follow lines on the floor. The more expensive may include sound and light detectors and even a speech synthesizer. Small robot arms can also be bought by the enthusiast, many of them small enough to sit on a desk. They are usually driven by electric motors but may be pneumatic (air driven) or even hydraulic (water driven) and can lift weights of about 1 kg (2 lb) or even more.

These robots can be bought in kit form and built at home. They can all move around, responding to simple commands.

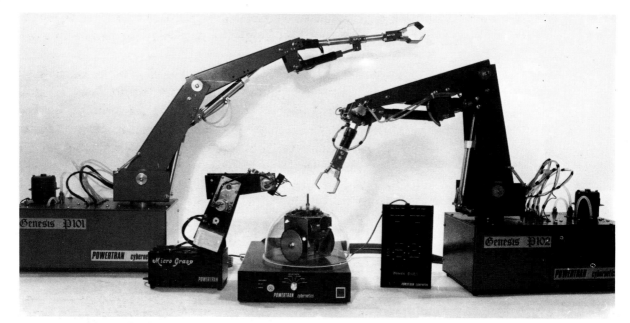

All that is needed to run a small robot at home is a microcomputer, an interface (through which the computer communicates its instructions to the robot), an extra power supply for the robot (a transformer or batteries), and the robot itself. Many of these small robots are available as kits. However, assembling the kits calls for some technical ability, or perhaps some expert help.

A good way to learn about robots is to construct kits like these. Here you can see three small desk-top robot arms and a turtle (third from the left).

What about the workers?

The last 200 years have seen machines steadily replacing human workers. As the heavy laboring jobs were replaced by machinery, people moved into lighter work, such as supplying machines with materials, or operating and supervising the machines. They also moved into administrative jobs and "service" jobs (such as nursing). People with jobs now put in only half as many hours as workers did a hundred years ago, and throughout the world there are millions of people who can no longer find jobs of any kind.

A new generation of intelligent robots, which do not need to be supervised or operated, may one day replace human workers. These new general-purpose robots could take over all kinds of manual work, even some highly skilled crafts. At the same time the computer will be replacing many office workers. It is possible that in future generations it will no longer be necessary for people to work at all!

Despite the fact that in the developed, industrialized countries, fewer people are working and for fewer hours, the standard of living has increased considerably in the past century. This is partly because a machine that is working produces wealth for society just as a working person does. There is every reason to believe that society will become even more productive, as robots begin to exploit resources in places people cannot reach – farming the seabeds or mining on other planets, say. As long as we can devise ways of sharing this new-found bounty fairly among people, a future of leisure and plenty may be only decades away.

This does not necessarily mean that people will be any happier, though. The prospect of a world without work fills many people with horror. They see human beings becoming like spoiled children, playing endless games while their robot servants pander to their needs. Perhaps this is what will happen, at least at first. But, given the time to think about their lives and to learn about themselves, it may be that people will at last discover what their true nature is, and be happier for the discovery.

Robots of the future will almost certainly not *look like this . . . but will real robots one day take over all the work now done by people?*

Glossary

Arm robot A type of robot that looks something like a human arm.

Artificial intelligence The field of research that tries to make computer programs that duplicate human thought processes. Also called Machine Intelligence.

Automata Machines that can perform complicated tasks but are not robots because they cannot be programmed to do useful work.

Computers Electronic devices for storing and manipulating information according to a program.

Envelope The area around a robot which it can reach with its "hand."

Feedback Information from a robot's sensors that tells the robot where it is and what is going on in the world around it.

Gripper A kind of robot "hand." Instead of grippers, a robot may have magnets or suction pads to hold things.

Hydraulics A method of powering a robot arm by pushing liquid under pressure into pistons.

Logo A programming language designed to move a small mobile robot such as a turtle.

Pneumatics A method of powering a robot arm by pushing air into pistons.

Program A set of instructions, usually stored in the computer, which tell the robot exactly what to do. Programs also tell the robot how to interpret the feedback from its sensors.

Robot A machine that can be programmed to do a useful job.

Robotics The science of designing and building robots.

Sensors Devices that take information about the world, turn it into electrical signals, and pass it to the robot's computer to be analyzed.

Turtle A type of small robot which moves on wheels.

Further reading

If you would like to find out more about robots, you may like to read the following books:

Billard, Mary. *All About Robots*. New York: Putnam, 1982.

Chester, Michael. *Robots: Facts Behind the Fiction*. New York: Macmillan, 1983.

Greene, Carol. *Robots*. Chicago, IL: Childrens Press, 1983.

Henson, Hilary. *Robots*. New York: Watts/ Warwick Press, 1982.

Knight, David C. *Robotics: Past, Present and future* New York: Morrow, 1983.

Litterick, Ian. *Robots and Intelligent Machines*. New York: Watts/Bookwright Press, 1984.

Marsh, Peter. *Robots*. New York: Watts/Warwick Press, 1984.

Rutland, Jonathan. *Exploring the World of Robots*. New York: Watts/Warwick Press, 1979.

Ryder, Joanne. *C-3PO's Book About Robots*. New York: Random House, 1983.

Silverstein, Alvin and Silverstein, Virginia. *The Robots Are Here*. Englewood Cliffs, NJ: Prentice-Hall, 1983.

Index

Acknowledgments

The publishers would like to thank all those who provided pictures on the following pages: David Anstey 13; Austin Rover 20, 30; BBC Hulton Picture Library 5; British Leyland 29; IBM 21; ML Aviation 32; Musee d'art et d'histoire, Neuchâtel (Switzerland) 7; PHOTRI 18, 23 (bottom), 33, 36, 37, 38, 39; Powertran Cybernetics Ltd. 44; Prism Consumer Products 40, 43; Rex Features *cover*, 4, 9, 17, 24, 25, 34, 35, 42, 45; Ann Ronan Picture Library 8; Science Photo Library 16, 23, 23 (top); Topham Picture Library 6, 28, 41; ZEFA 11, 12, 14, 15, 19, 27, 31. All other illustrations are from the Wayland Picture Library.